INCREDIBLE SPACE

Space
Stations

by Steve Kortenkamp

Reading Consultant:
Barbara J. Fox
Reading Specialist
North Carolina State University

Capstone

Mankato, Minnesota

Blazers is published by Capstone Press,
151 Good Counsel Drive, P.O. Box 669, Mankato, Minnesota 56002.
www.capstonepress.com

Library of Congress Cataloging-in-Publication Data
Kortenkamp, Steve.
    Space stations/by Steve Kortenkamp.
    p. cm. — (Blazers. Incredible space)
    Includes bibliographical references and index.
    Summary: "Discusses information about space stations within recent years as well as the
future of space stations" — Provided by publisher.
    ISBN-13: 978-1-4296-2323-0 (hardcover)
    ISBN-10: 1-4296-2323-3 (hardcover)
    1. Space stations — Juvenile literature. I. Title.
TL797.15.K67 2009
629.44'2 — dc22   2008029847

Editorial Credits

Abby Czeskleba, editor; Ted Williams, designer; Jo Miller, photo researcher

Photo Credits

Alamy/Carol and Mike Werner, 26
Getty Images Inc./National Geographic/Pierre Mion, 19; Time Life Pictures/NASA/Mark
    Dowman, 20
NASA, 5, 6, 10, 11, 12, 15, 16–17, 22, 28–29, cover; George Shelton, 9
Photo Researchers, Inc/Christian Darkin, 25
Shutterstock/argus (technology background), throughout; hcss5 (minimal code background
    vector), throughout

1 2 3 4 5 6   14 13 12 11 10 09

Table of Contents

chapter 1

Living in Space

An astronaut works on the *International Space Station* (*ISS*). She sees lights glowing on the nighttime Earth. But for this astronaut, the day has just begun.

International Space Station

a place for astronauts to live and work in space

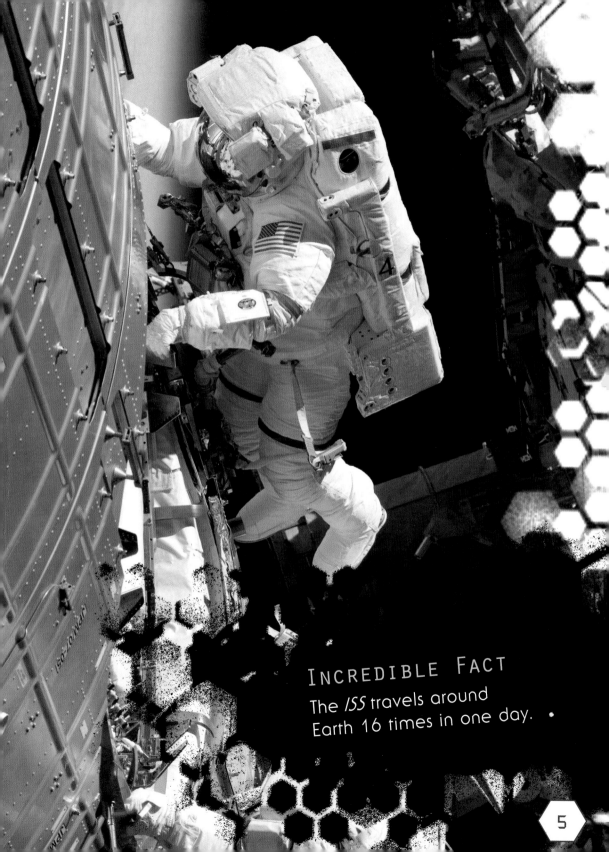

INCREDIBLE FACT

The *ISS* travels around
Earth 16 times in one day.

The United States and 15 other countries are building the *ISS*. Six astronauts will live on the *ISS* at one time. Someday, many more people may live in space.

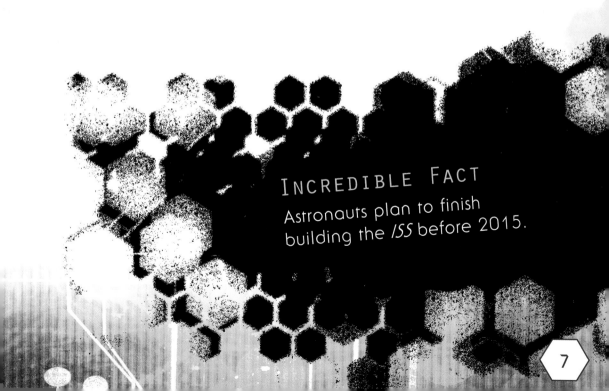

chapter 2

Building a Space Station

Around the world, engineers build pieces for the *ISS*. Planes fly the pieces to Kennedy Space Center in Florida. Workers carefully load the pieces inside space shuttles.

engineer
someone who designs and builds machines or buildings

The Columbus Laboratory is loaded onto a space shuttle at Kennedy Space Center.

A robot arm pulls equipment from the cargo bay of the space shuttle *Endeavour*.

Astronauts use shuttles to send new space station parts into space. A giant robot arm pulls the parts from the **cargo bay.**

cargo bay
the area in a space shuttle where large objects are stored and carried

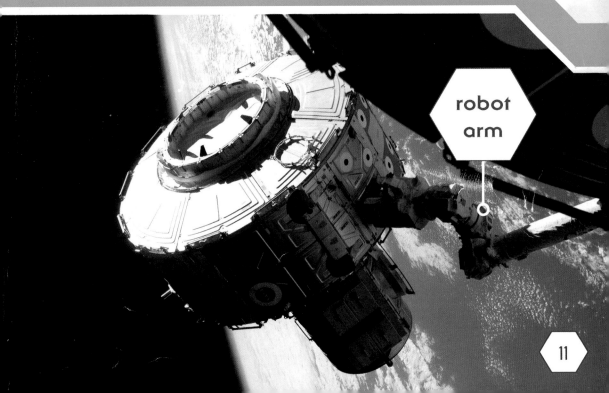

A robot arm adds a piece of equipment to the *ISS*.

robot arm

It feels like there is no **gravity** in space. This feeling makes heavy space station pieces seem light. Astronauts can easily use the robot arms to add big pieces to the space station.

gravity
a force that pulls objects together

The finished *ISS* will be bigger than a soccer field. It will be more than 100 feet (30 meters) tall.

ISS Diagram

robot arm

solar panel

cooling panel

Columbus
science lab

chapter 3

Preparing for Mars

In the future, astronauts will leave the *ISS* behind and go to Mars. The Mars trip will be more than 150 million miles (241 million kilometers) long.

INCREDIBLE FACT

It will take the astronauts six months to reach Mars.

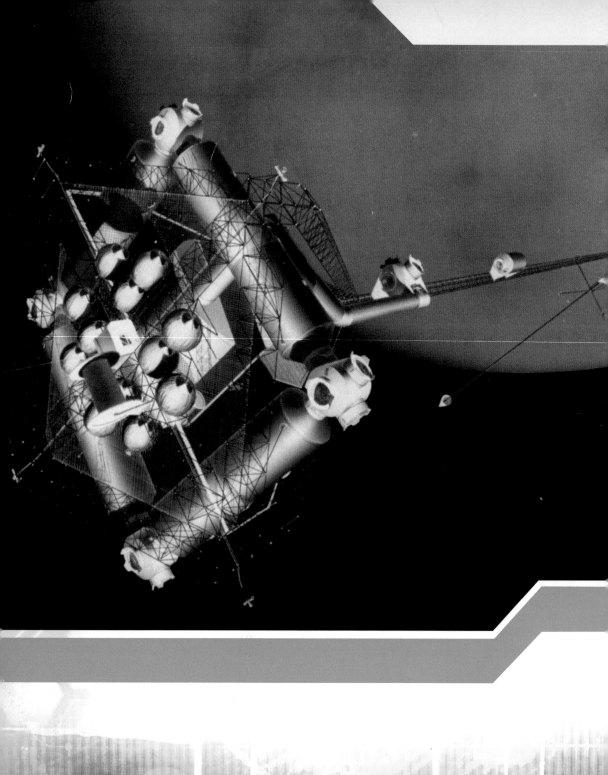

During the trip to Mars, astronauts will live in a new kind of space station. It will use big rockets and run on **nuclear power**.

nuclear power

energy created by breaking up atoms; atoms are the smallest parts of solids, liquids, and gases.

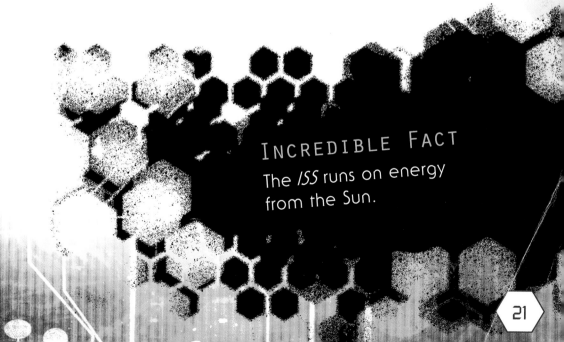

INCREDIBLE FACT

The *ISS* runs on energy from the Sun.

Astronauts must live in a space station on Mars. They cannot breathe the air on Mars. Astronauts may spend years studying the planet. Then they will return to Earth.

planet

a large object that moves around a star

chapter 4

Cities in Space

In the future, people may ride an elevator into space. The elevator will move on long **cables**. The cables will reach from Earth up to a space station.

cable

a thick wire or rope

INCREDIBLE FACT
Cables for space elevators will be more than 22,000 miles (35,406 kilometers) long.

There may one day be hotels in space.

Astronauts won't be the only ones riding elevators into space. People may be able to move their whole families into space. Space stations could one day become cities in space.

Working in Space

Glossary

cable (KAY-buhl) — a thick wire or rope

cargo bay (KAHR-goh BAY) — the area in a space shuttle where large objects are stored and carried

engineer (en-juh-NEER) — someone who designs and builds machines

equipment (i-KWIP-muhnt) — the machines and tools needed for a job or an activity

gravity (GRAV-uh-tee) — a force that pulls objects together

International Space Station (in-tur-NASH-uh-nuhl SPAYSS STAY-shuhn) — a place for astronauts to live and work in space

nuclear power (NOO-klee-ur POU-ur) — energy created by breaking up atoms; atoms are the smallest parts of solids, liquids, and gases.

planet (PLAN-it) — a large object that moves around a star

space shuttle (SPAYSS SHUT-ul) — a spacecraft that carries astronauts into space and back to Earth

Read More

Flammang, James M. *Space Travel.* Innovation in Transportation. Ann Arbor, Mich.: Cherry Lake, 2009.

Jefferis, David, and Mat Irvine. *Exploring Planet Mars.* Humans in Space. New York: Crabtree, 2007.

Zuehlke, Jeffrey. *The Space Shuttle.* Pull Ahead Books. Minneapolis: Lerner, 2007.

Internet Sites

FactHound offers a safe, fun way to find educator-approved Internet sites related to this book.

Here's what you do:

1. Visit *www.facthound.com*
2. Choose your grade level.
3. Begin your search.

This book's ID number is 9781429623230.

FactHound will fetch the best sites for you!

Index